NO POWER
on EARTH

FASTBACK® Horror

NO POWER on EARTH

Julia Remine Piggin

GLOBE FEARON
Pearson Learning Group

FASTBACK® HORROR BOOKS

The Caller
The Disappearing Man
Guts
Live Bait
The Lonely One
Mad Dog
The Masterpiece
Message for Murder
Night Games
Night Ride
No Power on Earth
Tomb of Horror

Cover photographer: Cameron Mitchell

Copyright © 1985 by Pearson Education, Inc., publishing as Globe Fearon, an imprint of Pearson Learning Group, 299 Jefferson Road, Parsippany, NJ 07054. All rights reserved. No part of this book may be reproduced or transmitted in any form or by any means, electronic, or mechanical, including photocopying, recording, or by any information storage and retrieval system, without permission in writing from the publisher. For information regarding permission(s), write to Rights and Permissions Department.

ISBN 0-8224-3776-7
Printed in the United States of America

11 12 13 14   06 05 04 03   **1-800-321-3106**
                                          www.pearsonlearning.com

My name is Bill Barlow. Last night I was just an ordinary guy. But I was probably happier than most guys. Maybe a little too happy. I'd just landed a dream job with a construction company in South America. It meant moving from country to country, meeting different people and seeing strange and exciting places. It was the kind of adventure Lisa and I had always said we wanted to have after we got married.

I took Lisa to dinner and told her the

good news. I asked her to marry me. We couldn't take much with us, but who cared? We had always said *things* didn't matter to us.

I expected her face to light up with joy and excitement. I'd known Lisa since we were juniors in high school. We had talked about a life together just like the one my new job would have given us. That's why I was completely puzzled when she looked at me with such a sad face.

"Bill," she said, "I want so much to marry you and for us to go away together. I want that more than anything in the world. But I can't. I love you. Don't follow me."

Then she jumped up and ran out of the restaurant.

The next morning our door bell rang very early. My parents were still asleep. I went downstairs to open the door. The young girl who delivers our newspaper was standing there beside her bike. She held out the paper and an envelope.

"Bill, Lisa Fisher asked me to give this to you," she said. Then she jumped on her bike and rode away.

I took the envelope upstairs and opened it. Inside was a long letter. I read it. And I couldn't believe it. This is what it said.

Dear Bill: I'm sorry I ran out so suddenly last night. I'm writing to say good-bye. I can't marry you. Not next week, not ever. Go to South America and forget about me. I wish I could just let it go at that. But I can't. Not after all the things we planned and talked about for years. I owe you an explanation.

So I'll tell you the whole story. I know now I should have told you about this a long time ago. I guess I was just hoping I wouldn't have to, that things would work out for us. But I see now I was being foolish. It's hopeless. After you read this, you probably won't believe it. But it's true, every word of it. Perhaps you'll think I'm crazy. Maybe that would be better. That way it would be easier for you not to see me again. Because you can't, Bill. Not ever. You can't save me. Please don't try.

It all began when I was 14, and my

great-aunt Rowena died. My father used to talk about her every once in a while. He claimed she was pretty strange. She never married, and lived for years in a huge, old mansion her family owned. When her parents died she just kept on living there, all alone. No one in my father's family ever saw or heard from her.

When she died she left all her money and possessions to her two surviving relatives—my father and his cousin John. Cousin John got most of the money (some of it went to charity), and my father got the "household effects." That made my father angry, knowing that his cousin, who was already rich, was becoming richer, while all he got was some "junky, old furniture."

Of course, it didn't take much to make my father angry. You never knew him, Bill, but he was a hard, bitter person for most of his life. He'd had health problems since he was young, and he spent a lot of time feeling sorry for himself. He could never hold onto a job for very long. Most of the time we were poor, and he made my mother's life pretty miserable.

Anyway, I'll never forget the day Aunt Ro's things were delivered. My father was lying on the sofa, as usual, claiming he felt sick, when the van pulled up outside. My mother shook him and said, "The things from your aunt are here."

My father just pushed his face farther into the pillow, and said, "I don't care."

The moving men carried a load of heavy

furniture up the three flights of stairs to our apartment. Most of it was very old, but very beautiful. There was even a polished rosewood piano. It all looked so out of place in the shabby apartment that we lived in.

Along with all the furniture and the piano was a painting. It was a portrait of a dark young man in a uniform with gold buttons. A sword hung at his side. And his dark eyes looked as if they followed you wherever you went.

I liked the painting right away. The young officer seemed to be smiling at me whenever I looked at it. Those eyes looked as if they enjoyed seeing me. I knew it was only a trick of the light, but it made me feel good.

My mother called Ralph Norstrand to help hang the portrait. Ralph lived one floor below us in our building. He was a very nice person, and he felt sorry for my mom and the hard life she had. He did all the work around our apartment that my father said he was too sick to do. My mother's face was always rosy and younger-looking whenever Ralph was around.

"I hope this holds," Ralph said, pounding a picture hook into the cracked wall. There was a snowfall of plaster. But he managed to slide the wire on the hook. It held. "I wouldn't stand too close to it," he told my mother. "If that heavy baby fell, it could do some damage."

My mother held his hand for a long time when she thanked him.

My father woke up about an hour later. "Where did all this stuff come from?" he asked, rubbing his eyes. "Oh, that's right, Aunt Ro's." He got up and went over to the piano. Bending down, he started to play a little tune, and began to sing:

*"When, oh when we meet again
No power on earth will part us then."*

He laughed.

"Don't know where I ever learned a corny old number like that," he said. He walked over and stood in front of the portrait.

"Hey, I remember this," he said. "When I was a kid they said it was worth a lot of money. I'll get some art dealer to tell us how much. But right now, I'll just drag it down to the pawn shop. We could use the cash."

"No!" My own voice surprised me. It sounded like someone else's voice coming from my mouth. "You can't pawn it! It's the only thing we've ever had that I loved!"

"Well, listen to who's giving orders around here now," my father said. "Look, Princess, I'll get it back tomorrow. Right now . . ."

"Oh, yes, I know how you get things back," my mother sneered. "Where's my watch? Where's my engagement ring? Kiss the picture good-bye, Lisa."

I ran and stood in front of the picture.

My father's face turned mean. He pushed me aside and reached up to lift the picture off the wall.

His hands never touched the frame. There was a flash of fiery red. The heavy painting seemed to leap from the wall. It hit my father on the head, knocking him down. He lay under it, but didn't make a sound.

My father was dead. And I was the only one who had seen the red flash—from the eyes in the picture.

The doctor said my father died from hitting his head on the floor when the painting knocked him down. Later I heard the doctor tell Ralph Norstrand that he couldn't explain the burn marks on my father's face and hands. My mother had said they certainly weren't there before the accident. I didn't say anything about what I'd seen.

I can't really say that we missed my father. I'm sure my mother loved him once, long ago, when they were first married. But after years of unhappiness, caused mostly by his laziness and meanness, I guess her love died. As for me, he had never paid much attention to me or taken any interest in what I did. He never seemed to know or care that I was even around. It's hard to miss someone who treats you that way.

My mother and Ralph Norstrand were married seven months after my father died. We moved into a clean new house just outside of town. The house I'm writing in, now. The house that I will never leave again.

Aunt Rowena's furniture looked perfect in the long, pleasant living room of our new house. The portrait hung at one end of the room. For a long time I couldn't look at it. I kept telling myself the whole thing with my father was just a crazy accident. The eyes in the painting still followed me. But they looked stern. Strange, somehow.

Things were better, though. Away from the slum and my father's problems, I had a new life. I had nicer clothes and made new friends. And I met you, Bill. I liked you from the first moment I saw you in math class. But if you remember, I almost never let you come into the living room when you called for me. Some of the excuses I made must have seemed silly. I made them because I was afraid.

You usually drove me home from school. But that day in the fall, when we were both 17, remember—I wanted to walk alone. I didn't tell you I had a feeling that something bad was going to happen. I knew I couldn't stop it. But I wanted to put it off as long as I could.

As I walked home a tune began to run through my head. You know how it is when you hear the notes in your mind, but can't think of what song it is. The tune seemed to grow louder. It began to fill the space around me. The dry leaves under my feet seemed to crackle to it. The branches of the trees rustled in time to it.

It was sunset, and the red sun seemed to be sinking to the rhythm of the tune. A cat ran up to me, meowing. It was meowing the muffled words to the tune.

The song was haunting the street. When I saw our house, pale in the dim light, I began to run. I had the feeling that something horrible was waiting there. And the song still seemed to be taking over the world around me.

I pushed my key into the lock, opened the door, and stepped into the hall. Sharp fingers, like a skeleton's, tore into my shoulders. The next thing I knew a blue face without features was pushed up against mine. I tried to scream, but a coarse-skinned hand was slapped over my mouth.

"Do what we say and you won't be hurt," an icy voice said, though the lips didn't move.

It dragged me into the living room. Another creature, whose flat featureless face was a sickly green, grabbed me and tied my hands behind my back. The blue-faced one pulled a rough piece of cloth from somewhere and gagged me.

I was numb with terror. But I quickly realized that these were not creatures from another world. They were human beings with stockings pulled over their heads. There were slits at the eyes so that they could see.

My mother's jewelry case was in the middle of the floor. Beside it was a bulging sack. I knew valuable things that belonged to my family were in it. I didn't really care. I only wanted to stay alive. Then I looked toward the end of the room, and I saw that the thieves had brought a little stepladder from the kitchen. It stood in front of the portrait of the officer.

Suddenly the song blared loud and clear in my mind. It was so loud that it seemed as if the burglars should be able to hear it. I knew what it was, now. It was the song my father had sung the day he died. I could not speak or move. But I could see. The face in the painting had changed. And it wasn't any trick of the light. The dark eyes were filled with hate. If I could have made a sound, I guess I would have warned the faceless thieves.

But I was helpless. The blue-faced thief moved toward the ladder. I shut my eyes, to block out the portrait's face. I had only to wait a second.

There was a swishing, hissing sound and a blue-white flash that I could see through my closed eyelids. The thief let out an unearthly scream. I opened my eyes. His left hand hung by a thread of flesh. I stared in horror. The portrait's eyes were wild, and its mouth was twisted. There was another flash, another sizzling hiss. The green-faced thief howled as the stocking was slashed and blood spurted from a terrible gash in the flesh beneath it.

The screams were horrible. I wanted to scream too. But I was gagged.

The thieves were lucky, in a way. Just then a squad car was passing the house. The policemen heard the terrible shrieks and broke in the door. The blue-faced thief didn't lose his hand. Surgeons stitched it back on, but it would be useless. The green-faced burglar turned out to be a girl. Her scar was too deep for plastic surgery to be of much help.

Neither of them could tell what had happened. The police guessed they must have gotten into a fight with the knives they carried. The thieves said that wasn't true. But who would believe them?

And who would have believed me, if I had told what I had seen? Do you believe me now, Bill?

At the time you knew there had been a robbery, and that I was sick afterward.

Now you know what I couldn't tell you then. But it wasn't the wild cries and the spurting blood that scared me most. It was what I saw when the thieves were gone and I looked at the portrait of the officer. The sword that hung at his side was no longer just the silver color of steel. Along one edge ran a thin line of red. As if it had cut quickly and neatly into flesh.

I tried not to look at the picture for a long time after that. But one night I woke up and heard the song again. It was all around me, filling my room. Something drew me down the stairs, into the living room, the song pounding loudly in the air. I stood in front of the portrait of the soldier. His eyes bored into mine. And the words of the song swirled and rang out in the room:

*"When, oh when we meet again
No power on earth will part us then."*

I knew why he had—there's only one word—"sent" for me. It was because of you, Bill. We were serious about each other, now. You'd asked me to marry you when you got a job. I said I wanted to go far, far away. Now you know why.

Last night, I ran home. My parents are away, so I—*we*—were alone in the house. I went into the living room and stood in front of—him. Your love had made me brave. I looked up at him, and said words I hadn't meant to say. And yet, I think I'd wanted to say them for a long time. "I'm alive and you're dead," I said.

Then, Bill, his eyes burned. And there was a swirling, sweeping force of some kind surging around me. It caught me, turned me around, and held me. I fought it—I grabbed at it and seemed to tear something away from it, and I beat at it with all my strength. And then it let me go. But I know it's only for a little while. Bill, he's killed and maimed because he might be taken away from me. Think what he'll do to somebody who wants to take *me* away. I know you can't believe this. Maybe what's in the envelope with this letter will make you believe enough to listen to me. Go, Bill, and try to forget you ever knew me. I love you. Good-bye.

Lisa

In the envelope was a button—a brass button from an old, old military uniform.

When I finished reading the letter, I just stood there in my room stunned. Lisa was right when she said I wouldn't believe her story. At first I didn't believe it. Would you?

Then I read the letter a second time. And I began to change my mind. It sounded crazy. But it explained a lot of the mystery about Lisa's past that she would never tell me. And there was one other thing. Why would she make up a story like that? I knew she wasn't crazy. I had known her too long and too well. And I was sure she loved me and wanted to marry me. So, the story *had* to be true. I had no choice but to believe it.

I knew what I had to do. If Lisa were to be free, the portrait must be destroyed. I got dressed and went out to the garage. I found a small ax, poured kerosene into a bottle, and stuffed a rag into its neck. I got in my car and drove as fast as I could to Lisa's house.

The front door was open. I went into the hall. It was a gray day. The hall was almost dark. But a strange, greenish light was coming from under the closed door of the living room. And there was cold air seeping out, too. I tried to tell myself that someone must have left a window open and a lamp on. But I knew better.

The ax was at my waist, hanging from the belt of my jeans. I held the bottle of kerosene in one hand and a match in the other. I stood there for a second, thinking. It wasn't too late. I could turn around and go home. I could pack, and next week I could get on the plane to South America—alone. I told myself that. Then I pushed the door open with my foot.

Lisa was standing in the center of the room. All around her was a curling mist. But from where I stood I could see the face in the painting—its mouth was twisted, its eyes were wild.

Lisa saw me and what I had in my hands. "Bill, don't!" she cried out.

I grabbed her and pushed her out the open door. Then I struck the match, lighted the rag, and hurled the bottle at the painted face. When it hit, flames shot out. I didn't wait to see the face burning.

I ran into the hall, took Lisa by the hand, and headed for the car. I opened the door on the driver's side, pushed her across the seat, and climbed in next to her. I drove off, not even thinking of where we were going. The important thing was that Lisa was free.

She was crouched down in the seat beside me, crying. Her hands covered her face. I reached down and pulled them away. "Lisa, look at me," I said.

She stopped crying and raised her head. And my blood turned to ice.

It wasn't Lisa's face that looked back at me. Nor her eyes. It was the face—and eyes—of the portrait.